U0059624

走出城堡的王子

William Arthur Philip Louis

威　廉　王　子　生　活　寫　眞

黛安娜王妃和剛出世的威廉

啣著金湯匙出生

　　一九八二年六月二十一日那天，在一個明麗夏日的薄暮時分裡，英國未來的國王——威廉‧亞瑟‧菲利浦‧路易斯，終於呱呱落地。這個初生的小傢伙有七英磅十盎司重，長著一頭捲曲的美麗金髮，還有一雙清澈碧藍的眼睛…

　　As dusk was falling at the end of a bright summer's day on June 21, 1982, the future king of England, William Arthur Philip Louis, gulped his first breath of air. The little lad weighed 71b 10oz and had a wisp of fair, blondish hair, and clear blue eyes....

一九八四年九月，威廉和查理親王一起在亞伯丁機場。

好奇寶寶

　　威廉是一個早熟的小孩，生活在奶媽溺愛的環護當中，他藉著與父母談話、玩耍學會了簡單的語彙，並且充滿了好奇心。一九八三年在巴爾摩洛的暑假期間，當時只有十五個月大的威廉，就曾經引起大騷動。當奶媽把他獨自留在育嬰室玩玩具，才一會兒的時間，他就認出了安裝在育嬰室牆上一枚吸引人的按鈕，然後按下它，把警報的信號傳送到亞伯丁警備總部。警察急速趕到了巴爾摩洛，立即封鎖了古堡和整個外圍庭園，等荷槍肅衣的警察大隊心急惶恐地推開育嬰室，卻只見到威廉露出一臉的無辜和童稚。

William was a precocious little child. Surrounded by his doting nanny,talked to and played with by his parents, he had an early vocabulary and was natually curious. During the 1983 summer holiday in Balmoral, when just fifteen months old, William was left to his own devices for just a few minutes and spotted a tempting button on the nursery wall. He pushed it, sending an alarm signal to the Aberdeen police headquarters. It wasn't until the police had raced to Balmoral, sealed off the castle and the entire grounds, that it was discovered that William had been responsible for the furore....

一九八六年八月，在巴爾摩洛的威廉和黛安娜。

小色狼

威廉五歲的時候，已經養成了捏他母親臀部，讓她嚇一跳的調皮習慣，通常，黛安娜都會笑著驚叫起來，因而鼓勵了她小兒子的這種行為。不過，威廉接著又去捏其他別女人的臀部，包括女侍、女僕侍，以及到肯辛頓宮拜訪黛安娜的女性友人。有一次，在一個學校的運動日裡，人家看到他捏了一個女人的臀部，黛安娜露出堅決反對之意，他就表現出有點威脅她的樣子。

一九八七年六月，吃著草莓冰淇淋的威廉。

He also loved teasing women, espe[cia]lly his mother. When he was five years-old, he developed a naughty habit of pinching her bottom, making her jump. Usually, Diana screamed with laughter, encouraging her young son. But then William began pinching other women's bottoms, including maids and servants and friends who came to visit Diana at Kensington Palace. Once, he was caught pinching a woman's bottom at a school sports day and Diana had to put her foot down. He was becoming a little menace. Staff at Highgrove have never forgotten the day when five-year-old William dug up a buried rabbit from the compost heap, swinging it around his head and yelling for his mother to look. He threatened to throw it at her but Diana's screams deterred him and he put the carcass back on the compost heap.

在馬球場上的威廉和黛安娜王妃

七歲的威廉王子，在溫莎大公園馬球比賽場上。

備受寵愛的袋熊

像大多數蹣跚學步的小孩一樣，威廉對每件事都感到興致盎然。他最討人喜愛的惡作劇，就是把任何手能抓到的東西，丟入抽水馬桶去，甚至連查理的鞋子也不能倖免。就像天底下所有的父母一樣，黛安娜和查理認為這些孩子氣的搗蛋行為都是蠻有趣可愛的，所以他們並沒有處罰這個小男孩，反而將他取了個「袋熊」（一種澳洲的小熊）的綽號。威廉王子是無條件的被寵愛著，令人無法相信的被縱容著，而且成為他父母世界裡的中心。

Like most toddlers, William was into everything. His favourites trick was flushing anything he could get his hands on down the loo, including his father's shoes. Like millions of parents before them, Diana and Charles found all this childlike mischief hilariously endearing and, instead of chastising the little boy, they nicknamed him Wombat (an Australian small bear). For the time being at least, Prince William was unconditionally adored, unbelievably pampered and the center of his parent's world....

一九九四年十月，威廉與波福狩獵隊（Beaufort Hunt）。

與生俱來的運動細胞

　　威廉喜愛各種運動，尤其偏好速度極快的。他從小就是一個熟練的騎馬師，可以輕易自如的從無鞍的小馬背跳上跳下，甚至還能立在他健壯的謝德蘭小馬的馬鞍上奔馳呢！五歲在威瑟比學校裡，他最擅長賽跑和跳高。八歲到了羅契洛夫就讀時，在足球場上他剛開始顯得有點猶豫，不過，經過鼓舞激勵之後，卻變成了一位優秀、甚至有攻擊力的球員，還被選為代表學校首度成軍的足球校隊。

　　William loved sport of any kind and preferably at the highest speed. He was an adept horseman from an early age, vaulting on and off his bareback pony with ease and even riding his sturdy Shetland pony while standing on the saddle! At Wetherby school, William excelled in running and the high jump. At Ludgrove, he was somewhat hesitant on the football field, but with encouragement he became a good, even aggressive, football, and was selected to play for the school's first team....

一九八八年四月，在海格洛夫的馴馬師摩理恩‧考克斯（Maureen Cox）陪同下學騎馬。

一九八七年四月在巴爾摩洛，淘氣的威廉王子將石頭丟入笛河（the river Dee）裡。

喜歡冒險的頑皮鬼

　　威廉已經長大成為一個叛逆、膽大的頑皮鬼了！他的身影不斷地穿梭樹林、翻爬籬笆、跨越鐵欄、攀爬圍牆，就算是受傷也不肯罷休，這對他已經是家常便飯了。他也喜歡爬樹，而且是愈高愈好，有時後，他的便衣侍衛還必須將他從五十尺高的樹上，一步步引導營救下來。大家都知道他常常受傷，然而，就在為疼痛哭完以後，他會再回到原來的遊戲上繼續玩，重新再冒一次險。

William was becoming something of a rebel as well as a dare-devil, earning a reputation for often getting into scrapes, running into trees, fences, iron bars and lumps of concrete. He also loved climbing trees, the taller the better. On occasions, his detective had to rescue him, guiding him down from trees fifty feet high. He was renowned for constantly hurting himself, though after a few tears he would return to whatever game he had been playing, taking the risks once again.

一九八九年威廉在馬球場上

愛打架的小孩

　　一九八五年九月的一個艷陽天，威廉穿著一雙紅短襪和格子裙迎接他的第一天上學日。在這個舒適的學校環境裡，威廉愉快的過著與大多數學齡前學生一樣的遊戲玩耍生活——畫畫、遊戲、作模型，同時也學數數，並且熟練基本的讀寫能力。不過這個聰明的小男孩——威廉，很快就學會如何依仗權勢欺凌其他小孩了。

On a sunny September day in 1985, William arrived for his first day at school wearing a pair of red shorts and a checked shirt.... In this cosy environment he enjoyed all the games and fun common to most pre-scholers-finger painting, water play and modelling, as well as learning to count and being introduced to the rudiments of reading and writing. A bright little boy, William quickly learned how to pull rank on the other children.

　　「如果你不聽我的話去做，我就把你逮捕起來，」這一句是在遊樂場最常被聽到的。他的貼身侍衛必須常常安撫小主人，但是，有時候威廉實在太機靈了，貼身侍衛稍有不慎時，他就和小同學打起架來了。因此，上學才幾個星期，威廉就被冠以「愛打架的小孩」的綽號。

' If you don't do what I want I'll have you arrested,' was one phrase which could be often heard echoing around the playground. His assigned bodyguard often had to calm down his young charge, but sometimes Wills was too quick for him and a fight would have started in the time it took for the bodyguard to look away. Within weeks, William had been nicknamed ' Basher'.

一九八六年七月，調皮的威廉王子在安德魯王子和莎拉‧佛姬的婚禮上對群眾揮手。

調皮搗蛋的小花童

　　一九八六年莎拉‧佛姬與安德魯王子的婚禮，威廉王子在婚禮上當花童，其他的小孩在整個典禮過程中，都表現得非常規矩，只有威廉一人簡直是個小禍星。他在整個婚禮宣誓典禮過程中，非常地急躁不安，還對小伴娘吐舌頭作鬼臉，就像一般頑皮搗蛋的小男孩一樣。這一次，電視攝影人員捕捉到了他刁鑽古怪的鏡頭，這樣的尷尬，令查理爸爸相當惱怒。

Charles was especially upset by his son's behaviour at the wedding of Sarah Ferguson to Prince Andrew in 1986. Prince William was a page boy, but whilst the other children were models of good behaviour throughout the ceremony, William was a disaster. He fidgeted throughout the vows, stuck his tongue out at the young bridesmaids and generally behaved like a naughty little boy. This time, the TV cameras captured his antics and Charles was extremely upset.

一九八六年七月，在婚禮上水手裝扮的威廉王子。

一九九二年七月，在英國格蘭匹茲大賽車（British Grand Prix）會場上。

On June 3, 1991, he was playing golf with friends at the school when one of them accidentally hit him a crashing blow to the head with an iron club. William collapsed, knocked unconscious with blood pouring from the wood. By the time he reached the casualty department of the Royal Berkshire Hospital, a distraught Diana and Charles were by his side. As doctors examined the wound and pronounced it to be serious.... Diana accepting the advice of the senior doctor present, insisted that he go to Gt Ormond Street Hospital for Sick Children.....she sat in the ambulance with William as it raced towards London, accompanied by police car and motorcycle outriders.

意外傷害

　　一九九一年六月三日，威廉在學校與同學打高爾夫球，當時其中一位同學不小心用鐵桿重擊到他頭部，他當場昏迷倒地，血不斷從傷口湧出來。他及時的被送到皇室博克夏醫院意外傷害科診斷急救，當時極為憂慮不安的黛安娜和查理在旁看顧著他。當醫生檢查過傷口，宣佈情況嚴重！黛安娜接受了在場資深醫生的建議，把他送到葛瑞特歐蒙街兒童醫院去。她和威廉坐在救護車裡，由警車和外圍摩托車隊護送，飛速開往倫敦。

一九九六年三月，威廉在伊頓一場足球賽中，重重摔了一跤。

一九九一年與黛安娜在卡地夫的聖大衛節日（St. David's Day）上

William Arthur Philip Louis

William Arthur Philip Louis

母子情深

對威廉來説,與哈利、母親在肯辛頓宮的生活,總是充滿了歡笑、樂趣。威廉喜歡早晨的時候跑進他母親的臥房,鑽進被窩裡摟抱她,然後一邊玩玩具一邊叫著笑成一團。他向來喜歡和母親打枕頭仗,每當他準備用枕頭打他母親的臉,或者當哈利和他母親聯合戰線攻擊他的時候,他就會模仿可怕的尖叫聲攻擊他們。

For William, life at Kensington Palace, with Harry and his mother, was so often full of laughter and fun. William loved to run into his mother's bedroom in the morning, give her a cuddle in bed and play with toys, with all of them laughing and shouting at the same time. He used to enjoy the pillow fights with his mother screaming in mock horror whenever he managed to hit her in the face with a pillow or when Harry would join his mother in the fight against him.

一九九七年八月（威廉母親悲劇死亡前兩個星期），他和父親、哈利在巴爾摩洛渡假。

崇拜父親

七歲的時候，威廉開始喜歡有關恐龍、行星、太空旅行、野生動物，還有危險有毒的小蟲和昆蟲的錄影帶。威廉會常常跑去問他父親許多千奇百怪的問題，無論是關於地理、野生動物、恐龍、其他國家，或是星星是如何持續不變的停留在天空中等等的問題。

By the age of seven, William loved watching videos about dinosaurs, planets, space travel, planets, space travel, wild animals and dangerous, poisonous bugs and insects. Wills would often go to his father for answers to all the hundreds of questions he had, whether it was about geography, wild animals, dinosaurs, other countries or how the stars stayed up in the sky.

他也發現到父親是個好同伴，特別是在巴爾摩洛他們一起外出時，因為父親對於馬術和打獵、射擊和釣魚、逐鹿，以及對鄉間的知識非常豐富；一年一年的，他發現自己愈來愈接近父親查爾斯親王，他希望有一天也會精通這些知識，並且能善加運用。此外，他也仰慕他父親在千百人前，能從容穩健、毫不膽怯的演說態度，他孩子氣地擔心著，有一天自己是否也能有同樣的自信發表演說。

He also discovered his father was great company when they went outdoors together, particularly at Balmoral. He came to realise that his father was very knowledgeable about horses and hunting, shooting and fishing, stalking deer and understanding the countryside and each year he found himself becoming closer to Prince Charles, hoping that one day he would be as skilled in the knowledge and practices of the countryside. And he admired the way his father could make speeches before hundreds of people without being shy or embarrassed and he wondered in his boyish insecurity whether, one day, he, too, would be able to deliver such speeches with the same confidence.

一九九五年八月，在倫敦抗日勝利日（VJ Day）第五十週年紀念的慶祝會上。

保護家人

　　威廉非常保護哈利，如果哈利與學校同學有了麻煩糾紛，他會跑去找威廉幫助。威廉就會立即作回應，警告其他小朋友說，若是他們膽敢取笑或欺負他弟弟，他就會要他們好看。因為威廉在學校所建立起來的名聲之故，同學就特別留意了他的警告。這樣的幫忙協助，漸漸促成了威廉和哈利之間密不可分的兄弟情誼。

　　William also became very protective towards Harry when he joined him at Ludgrove and, if Harry found himself in trouble with any of his school friends, he would run to William for help. In an instant, William would respond, warning the other youngsters that he would become involved if they dared to tease or bully his younger brother. And because of the reputation Wills had built up at the school, his warnings were heeded. Such help and assistance forged a strong bond between Wills and Harry…

　　就如同威廉嚐試要保護他弟弟那樣，從十歲起，他也想要保護他母親。有一天他告訴黛安娜說：「我長大後要成為一名警察。」她問他為什麼，威廉回答說：「這樣我就可以理所當然的保護你啊。」然而，哈利立即就粉碎了威廉騎士風度的抱負，對他哥哥說：「你不能當警察，你必須當國王。」

　　Just as William sought to protect his younger brother, so, from ten years of age, William wanted to protect his mother. One day he told Diana, 'When I grow up I'm going to be a policeman.' When she asked him why, Wills replied, 'So that I can look after you, of course.' Harry, however, promptly ruined Wills chivalrous ambition, remarking, 'You can't be a policeman. You've got be a king.'

一九九一年七月，黛安娜王妃與威廉在溫布頓觀看比賽。

羅契洛夫預校

王子渴望平凡的生活

威廉會為爭取像沒有特權的其他小孩那樣被對待而奮鬥。他不喜歡他的貼身侍衛必須從早到晚注意著他，因此有時會故意想辦法脫離他們的警界視線。藉著一些同學的協助，他們會設法將威廉藏在學校的某個地方，或操場校園裡，讓侍衛找不到威廉。於是立即就造成了驚慌的場面——特別是在貼身侍衛當中；但是他似乎一點也不在乎受到指責。他渴望這幾分鐘的獨處，可以在沒有貼身侍衛緊密的注意下，做他想做的事。

William fought to be treated like any other boy with no privileges. He didn't like the fact that his personal detectives had to keep watch over him day and night. Occasionally William would deliberately try to lose them. With the help of some friends, they would contrive to make Wills disappear, hiding him somewhere in the school or in the school grounds. That would cause immediate consternation, particularly amongst his bodyguards, but he didn't seem to care a damn. For a few minutes he was alone, able to do whatever he wanted without the close attention of one or more detectives....

William Arthur

一九九四年七月，和他母親在溫布頓觀看女子網球決賽。

Philip Louis

與母親的快樂時光

在肯辛頓宮和他母親單獨一起時，對威廉來說生活過得輕鬆休閒多了。黛安娜會安排他參觀博物館、藝廊、劇院或遊樂公園，也會讓威廉參加他擅長的小賽車，表現他過人的膽量和熟練的技巧。在夏季學期裡，威廉和黛安娜會在健身俱樂部練網球，也常常參加俱樂部的一些專業課程訓練。威廉和他母親有時候也一起去游泳，他非常喜歡和她在水中嬉戲玩鬧——將黛安娜浸到水裡、向她潑水以及與她游泳比賽。

At Kenshington Palace, life was far more relaxed for William, alone with his mother. Diana would try to arrange a visit to a museum, art gallery, cinema or amusement park, arrange for go-kart racing at which Wills excelled, showing great daring and skill. In the summer term, Diana and Wills might practice tennis at his mother's health club and William would often have some lessons with the club professional. Wills and his mother would sometimes go swimming together and he enjoyed fooling around with, ducking her, splashing her and trying to race her.

威廉與教練賈基・史都華在一輛一級方程式賽車的駕駛座上。

一九九二年二月，在卡地夫阿姆斯公園（Cardiff Arms Park），當時心情顯然很愉快的樣子。

靈活敏捷的運動員威廉，帶著手傷在伊頓參加橄欖球比賽。

足球小神童

在羅契洛夫小學就學期間，威廉才學會踢足球，並且愛上這項運動。在足球比賽時，威廉又再顯露了他的攻擊力，贏得了好成績。他在球場上抱球奔馳，艱苦奮鬥，還有能力在混戰當中維護到自己的安全。假日裡，他也會說服奶媽蒂姬一起踢足球，而哈利也會跟隨在後面跑。在羅契洛夫最後一年，威廉曾以無比的光榮擔任左後衛球員，代表校隊出賽其他校隊。

It was at Ludgrove that William learned how to play football, and he fell in love with the game. It was during football matches that Wills once again revealed his aggression, winning 50-55balls, making hard tackles and was quite capable of looking after himself in any mêlée. During the holidays, he would persuade Tiggy to play football and Harry would tag along, too. In his final year at Ludgrove, William took great pride in representing the school at left full-back in matches against other schools...

鄉居的威廉和他的拉布拉多獵犬（Labrador puppy）。

與王子擦肩而過

　　威廉和他的同學在溫莎城區閒逛時，他都會盡量保持低調。當然，一開始他看起來和午後外出的任何伊頓學生沒兩樣，不過在他逐漸成長後，他的形像比以往更容易被認出來，就有更多的市民會在街頭偶遇這位隨時帶著微笑，身高六呎、英俊金髮的年輕人，而認出他就是威廉——王位繼承人。有些居民會擦身而過，然後用溫和的聲音對他說：「祝好運」，但是由於聲音太小，以致沒有引起別人特別的注意。威廉通常會回答說：「謝謝」，然後繼續往前走，因為他的侍衛曾告誡他，在這樣的場合不可停下來和任何人說話。然而，到了威廉十六歲時，他比以前更容易被認出來，而觀光客就變得更加的大膽了。

For the most part, William retained his anonymity while walking around Windsor with his pals. Of course, he looked no different from any other young Eton scholar out for the afternoon, but as he grew older and his looks became more recognizable, more townspeople would have a second glance at the handsome, fair-haired, six-foot-tall young man with the ready smile, and realise that the young man was, indeed, William, the heir to the throne. Some townspeople would walk past and, say 'good luck' in a quite voice so as not to attract attention. William would usually reply with a 'thank you' and keep on walking, for he had been advised by his bodyguards not to stop and talk to anyone on such occasions. Tourists, however, became far more adventurous as William's sixteenth birthday loomed and he became that much more recognisable.

一九九五年九月，威廉在伊頓中學的第一天。

王子的中學課程

　　伊頓課程裡授有世界各地的語言，包括拉丁文、古典希臘文、阿拉伯文、中國官話（國語）、中文和日文，還有現代歐洲各國語言，不過課程裡也提供了其他的應用科目，例如藝術、音樂、電腦、烹飪和汽車維護。威廉選擇了踢英式足球和划船，不過伊頓生也可以玩橄欖球、板球、網球、壁手球和回力網球，還有著名的伊頓足球（一種對方攻擊時圍起一道牆防禦的球賽）。這些古怪的遊戲已經有幾十年沒有比賽的記錄了！伊頓的校服完全不像其他一般英國公學的校服，男孩們每天都穿著黑色燕尾服、背心、細條紋長褲，還套著一個白硬領子，不過他們還可以穿著便服走進溫莎城區。伊頓中學共有一千兩百六十位男學生，他們一起住在二十四間房間，每間容納五十位男孩的校舍裡。每年學費要花一萬兩千五百英鎊，額外費用加起來一年總額達一萬五千英鎊！

Eton taught most subjects under the sun, including Latin, classical Greek, Arabic, Mandarin, Chinese and Japanese, as well as the modern European languages. But lessons are also provided in other subjects such as art, music, computer studies, cookery and car maintenance. William chose to play soccer and to row, but Etonians can also play rugby, cricket, tennis, fives and racquets, and well as the famous Eton Wall Game, a contest in which a wall is defended while the opposition attacks. There has been no score in this odd game for decades! The uniform at Eton is like no other in any British public school. The boys wear black tail-coats, a waistcoat, pinstriped trousers and a stiff white collar every day. When they walk into Windsor, however, they are allowed to wear ordinary, casual clothes. William is one among 1,260 boys (there are no girls at Eton) who live in twenty-four houses accommodating about fifty boys each. Fees cost £12,500 a year, but extras bring that total to around £15,000 a year!

一九九八年三月，與查理親王和哈利在加拿大渡假。

哈利和威廉在「切爾西海灣健身院」（Chelsea Harbour gym）看完網球賽後離開。

一九九五年八月，在抗日勝利日慶祝會上觀看行進隊伍通過。

威廉在哈利王子七歲生日一星期之後，與他合拍的照片。

43

一九九一年在奧地利列許（Lech）的滑雪坡道上

一九九一年三月，威廉在卡地夫（Cardiff）第一次「走訪民眾」的步行儀式。

一九九五年四月，在海格洛夫附近的泰伯里村博覽會（Tebury Villiage Fair）上碰運氣。

傾慕

　　一九九五年六月，威廉度過十三歲生日之後的某個時期，他開始注意到女孩子。身為一個向來有些早熟傾向的小孩，而且就像許多小男孩一樣，威廉也被同年紀的女孩引發了好奇與興趣。不過，從威廉青少年時期起，他就漸漸對異性產生了更為濃厚的興趣和迷惑。

　　Some time after his thirteenth birthday, in June, 1995, William discovered girls. As a young child he had always been somewhat precocious and, like many young boys, intrigued by girls of his own age. But from the start of his teenage years, William developed a far greater interest and fascination with the opposite sex.

一九九五年四月，在倫敦騎士橋（Knightsbridge）街旁的花攤上買花，作為他母親的生日禮物。

搖滾威廉

　　威廉只有與母親在一起時，才會顯現出十三歲少年的熱衷與興趣。他喜歡動作片電影、科幻小說和搖滾樂團——像「槍與玫瑰」和「邦喬飛」。他喜歡穿黑牛仔褲、黑T恤、轟炸員夾克和教練裝⋯這些學校不允許他穿，或與他父母公開出現時不能穿的衣服。

　　But it was with his mother that Wills showed his teenage interests as he approached his thirteenth birthday. He liked action movies, science fiction and rock bands like Guns and Roses and Bon Jovi. He liked wearing black jean, black T-shirts, bomber jackets and trainers, everything that he was not allowed to wear at Ludgrove or when appearing in public with his parents....

王子的偶像

在威廉櫥櫃裡貼的照片是「海灘遊俠」的女主角潘蜜拉‧安德森和名模辛蒂‧克勞馥。其他令他櫥櫃增光不少的明星還包括名模克勞蒂‧雪佛和辣妹合唱團艾瑪‧邦汀。大家都知道他喜歡花花公子的封面女郎——雙胞胎夏恩和西雅‧芭比。有一回，威廉咯咯笑著，並且用手肘輕輕碰他的同學要他注意看時，他召喚他的貼身侍衛，也過來觀看這幅非常性感模樣的女郎照片。黛安娜卻用力將照片撕成兩半，遞給威廉和他學友每人各一半。威廉卻面無表情的告訴她說，「我們只要照片的上半部份。」

Inside William's locker are photos of *Baywatch's* babe Pamela Anderson and Cindy Crawford. Other stars to have graced his locker include Claudia Schiffer, and Emma 'Baby Spice' Bunting. From the age of thirteen he would always flick through his mother's magazines, which included both *Vogue* and *Cosmopolitan*. He was known to fancy the Playboy models, twins Shane and Sia Barbi, who are the living image of Barbie dolls. On one occasion, giggling and nudging a school pal, William summoned his bodyguard to survey a picture of a very sexy looking model. Diana sportingly tore the photo in half, handing William and his friend half each. Deadpan, William told her, ' It was only the top halves we wanted.'.......

一九九八年三月，
威廉在皇室訪問
加拿大期間，與父親在
維斯勒（Whistler）滑雪。

威廉愛的初體驗

　　一九九六年冬季在克羅斯特的滑雪假期間，威廉在滑雪坡道上和一個迷人的少女聊了起來，而且似乎被迷住了。過了一會兒，他們就一起滑雪，威廉還建議他們坐滑雪纜車返回坡頂，重新再滑一次。他也邀請她一起吃午餐。不過，這個女孩在第二天就離開了，而且彼此不再見過面。那個時候，威廉比她還小五歲呢！在同一次的滑雪旅行中，威廉也深深留意到了另一個令人著迷的少女──十八歲的柔伊・柯蒂辛普森，一位將軍的女兒。這位像極了黛安娜的柔伊也被邀請加入皇室滑雪隊，並且與他們共進午餐。有兩天的時間，柔伊和威廉一塊兒滑雪，似乎玩得很開心，威廉將她視為貴族後裔一樣談天說笑著。

During winter skiing at Klosters in 1996, Wills began chatting to an attractive teenage girl while on the slopes and seemed smitten. For a while they skied together and Wills suggested they return on the ski-lift for another down hill run. He invited her for a bite of lunch, too. But the girl was leaving the following day and they never saw each other again. At the time William was five years her junior! During the same ski trip, Wills was much taken with another teenager, the stunning 18-year-old Zoe Cody -Simpson, the daughter of an Army General. Zoe, who had more than a passing resemblance to Diana, was invited to join the royal skiing party and take lunch with them. For two days, Zoe and William skied together and both seemed to have great fun, William smiling and chatting as though to the manor born.

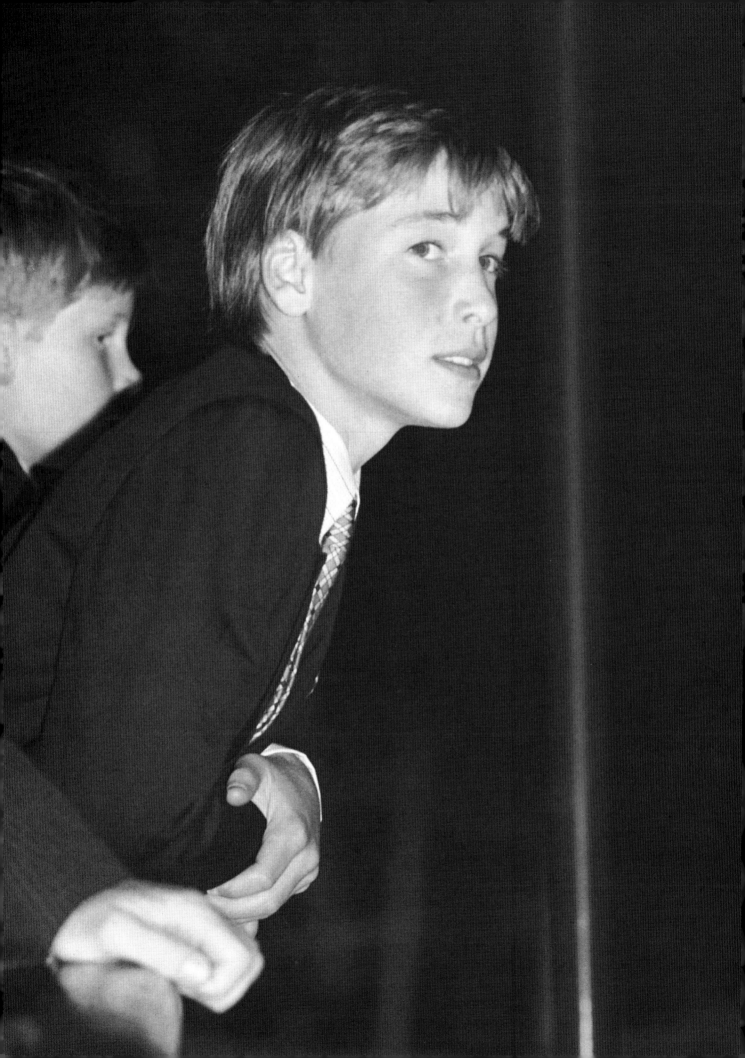

拒絕拍照的小子

　　有一回在巴爾摩洛笛河岸邊與父親、哈利的重要場合，威廉淡淡的表示不想作姿態給人拍照。在那個時候，父親要威廉與他一起合照，他以嚴厲的表情示意，極力說服威廉過來參與，但是當時的威廉很明顯的表現出一點也不快樂的樣子。當查理親王堅持要威廉過來照相，威廉聽從了（不過大多時候他會拒絕），結果新聞記者拍下來送回報社的照片，多半發現到品質效果極差。表面上，笛河岸邊的新聞照似乎顯示出一個帶著自然笑容，心情愉快的修長青年威廉。事實卻是，成群攝影記者所拍攝出來無以計數的膠捲中，只有少數幾個從中挑選出來的畫面，是人們想要看到的。

　　During one famous photo call on the banks of the River Dee at Balmoral with his father and Harry, William made it very plain that he had no intention of posing for pictures. On that occasion, his father asked him to pose with him, giving him stern looks in an effort to persuade him to come and join the photo call, but William made it very obvious that he was not at all happy. When Prince Charles insisted that he come and pose for the shoot, William obeyed, but most reluctantly, and, as a result, the photographs the pressmen sent back to their offices were of a poor quality. Superficially, the photocall on the hanks of the Dee appeared to show William as a cheerful, gangly youth with a ready smile. The reality was that only a handful of frames from countless rolls of film shot by the assembled photographers showed what everyone wanted to see.

黛安娜王妃的棺木抵達了西敏寺

當悲劇傳來

　　當威廉母親不幸的悲劇發生時，他和哈利、查理親王、女王以及菲利浦親王正在蘇格蘭巴爾摩洛度假。這樁在巴黎塞納河畔阿拉瑪橋底隧道內，震驚世人的意外車禍發生時，英國正值夏天，時間是一九九七年八月三十一日星期日晚上十一點半。

　　Prince William was holidaying at Balmoral in Scotland with Harry, Prince Charles, the Queen and Prince Philip, when the tragic death of his mother occurred. The appaling crash in the tunnel beneath the Pont de PAlma beside the River Seine in Paris happened at 11.30 pm British summer time on Sunday, August 31.1997.

威廉母親去世五天後，他和哈利、查理親王走出肯辛頓宮的大門外。

William

菲利浦親王、威廉、史賓塞伯爵、哈利王子和查理走在黛安娜靈柩行列的後面，前往舉行喪禮儀式的西敏寺。

一九九七年七月，在聖卓佩茲駕駛水上噴射摩托車（威廉和他母親最後度過的假期）。

運動家威廉

威廉是一位優秀的運動員。他喜歡很多的運動，包括划船、足球和水上馬球。他玩過橄欖球，不過這個冬季運動還不如足球那樣令他喜歡。他也喜歡打網球和壁球，在這兩種運動上，他表現出了相當特殊的才能，他的身高、強壯有力的體格賦予他這個優點，讓他勝過了同年齡的男孩。他也是一位技術精湛的滑雪手，而且堪稱是滑雪坡上的膽大鬼，現在已經可以在瑞士的克羅斯特、美國科羅拉多州亞斯本和加拿大等滑雪勝地，最險峻的離道滑雪坡上追上父親了，他喜歡滑下坡時快速追逐的挑戰。

William is already a natural athlete. He enjoys a number of sports, including rowing, football and water polo. He has played rugby but doesn't enjoy that winter sport as much as football, in which he has shown real talent. William also plays tennis and squash, two sports where he has shown quite exceptional talent, his tall, powerful physique giving him an advantage over boys of his own age. He is also a competent skier and has become quite a daredevil on the slopes, now outpacing his father on some of the most difficult off-piste slopes at Klosters in Switzerland, Aspen, in Colorado, USA, and in Canada. He loves the challenge of racing downhill...

一九九八年在加拿大，威廉心情愉快的接受人們的愛慕之情。

最佳服裝代言人

　　威廉他自己相當懂得穿著，在美國「時人雜誌」的「1996
年最佳服裝代表人物」中，編輯寫道：「他的穿著打扮看起來
就像是模特兒，可以說是完美無瑕。」威廉表現出來敏銳的穿
著判斷力，可以說涵蓋了他生活的各個層面，不管是穿著像他
父親一樣古典的英國格子裙和短靴，平常裝扮時設計風格的T
恤、牛仔褲和運動鞋，或者滑雪時穿的別緻鮮明的滑雪裝。當
然，威廉一直都很喜歡母親多年來對他機靈應變的引導。現在
保留下來可以看到的，不管是否已發展成他自己獨特的風格，
兼具了好品味和訣竅，都讓他不論穿什麼看起來都非常得體。

He knows how to dress. In the American *People magazine's*
'Best Dressed People of 1996' the editors wrote, 'He looks and
dresses like a model. He makes no mistakes.' And William's dress
sense covers every facet of his life, whether he is dressing in
classical English tweeds and brogues like his father, designer T-
shirts, jeans and sneakers when wearing casual apparel or dressing
with style and colour when skiing. Of course, William enjoyed his
mother's astute guidance for many years. It remains to be seen
whether he will now develop his own inimitable style, coupled with
good taste and a knack of always looking good in whatever he
wears.

一九九七年八月，在蘇格蘭巴拉特（Ballator）拍的新聞照片。

William Arthur Philip Louis

一九九六年在泰晤士河上

成為偶像

　　威廉首度成為偶像人物，是一九九七年十一月參加慶祝他皇室祖父母結婚五十週年紀念，在皇家海軍學院舉行的午宴所顯示出來的。當時有六百位少女高聲尖叫著他的到達，使得參與午宴的其他人大感驚訝。沒有人看過小威廉的出現有這樣的激烈反應，警察也大吃一驚，因為沒有想到會有這樣的尖叫歡迎儀式。

　　The first sign that William was becoming a cult figure, perhaps even an object of desire among the teenagers, was in November, 1997, When he attended a lunch at the Royal Naval College in Greenwich, celebrating his grandparents' 50th wedding anniversary. Six hundred screaming teenage girls heralded his arrival, much to the surprise of everyone else attending the lunch. No one had seen such a reaction to the youthful William's appearance and even the police were taken aback for no one was expecting such a screaming reception.

　　事實上，威廉可能成為「海報男孩」最早的跡象，是出現在一九九五年十月偶像熱門音樂雜誌Smash Hits印行的一張威廉男孩海報上，照片中的威廉穿著粗野鮮明的運動上衣和灰色長褲，還繫著領帶。結果海報全銷售一空。五個月後，威廉收到了五十四張情人卡，一年之後，他共收到超過五百張的情人卡。到了一九九八年，他已經收到一千張了！

　　In fact, the first signs that Prince William might become a pin-up occurred two years earlier, in October, 1995, when *Smash Hits* published a poster of a boyish William dressed in uncool blazer, tie and grey trousers. It was a sell-out. Five months later, William received 54 Valentine cards; a year later he had more than 500. In 1998, he received more than 1,000!

一九九七年六月，威廉王子15歲。

一九九八年三月在加拿大溫哥華。

最有價值的單身貴族

　　光陰似箭，歲月如梭，威廉王子已從一個青澀害羞的小男孩，蛻變成一位備受少女們青睞的自信少年了。這些少女對他心儀崇拜的程度，並不亞於一位受歡迎的超級偶像巨星。但她們並不認為威廉如那些Super Star般遙不可及，反而覺得他承自母親黛安娜親和的獨特魅力，有著鄰家男孩般的親切感。她們甚至幻想有朝一日可以和威廉約會，進而走進禮堂飛上枝頭當鳳凰！

　　Overnight almost, Prince William has matured from a shy young boy to a self-assured sixteen year old and teenage girls have taken note. They have become attracted to him in the same way as they would a new young pop star who suddenly emerged on the scene. They appear not to think of William as the heir to the British throne, a young man with the demands of future sovereignty on his mind, but rather as an accessible young man in exactly the same way as their mothers felt that Princess Diana was one of them, a woman apart from royalty who had the same problems as many women. Now, their teenage daughters feel that William is one of them as accessible and approachable as any pop-star or film star might be, someone they can dream about at night and fantasise that one day perhaps they might date.

一九九七年六月與查理親王在溫莎的馬球賽會場上。

一九九八年三月在加拿大溫哥華，陷在歡呼擁簇的群眾當中。

一九九七年七月，在女王的母親九十七歲慶生會上。

一九九七年六月，和伊頓學友在馬球比賽的護柵看台上。

即將告別伊頓中學

　　威廉會在伊頓中學獲得A-levels的成績畢業，而且如果順利的話，他期望進入牛津或劍橋大學就讀。查理親王是劍橋畢業的，但是黛安娜的弟弟查爾斯則是牛津莫德林學院的畢業生。眾人期待的最後決定，會在聽取負責教導威廉的伊頓師長們的意見後才會知道。大學之後，威廉可能會花一段時間受軍事訓練——陸軍、皇家海軍或皇家空軍。然而，他也可能會和父親一樣，在皇家空軍軍隊學開飛機，然後再轉移到皇家海軍。這一切只等待時間來解答。

William will take his A-levels at Eton and, if successful, he is expected to go to Oxford or Cambridge. Prince Charles went to Cambridge but Diana's brother, Charles, went to Magdalen College, Oxford. It is excepted that the final decision will be taken at the time on the advice of those Eton masters who have had responsibility for William's education. After university, William is likely to spend some time in one of the services; Army, Royal Navy or Royal Air Force. He might, however, like his father, learn to fly with the RAF and then move to the Royal Navy. Only time will tell.

一九九七年，威廉和父親在巴爾摩洛笛河岸邊。

翩翩美少年

　　隨著年齡的增長，威廉愈見英姿煥發，他不但英俊帥氣且笑容可掬，全身上下散發出一股親切優雅的獨特魅力。他對人謙和、友善、彬彬有禮，應對進退充分表現出皇室的高貴出眾，加上他與生俱來的羞赧氣質，相當受到民眾的喜愛。

Prince William is not only good-looking but he also has the easy, warm smile of his mother which devastates people he meets. He is an attractive young man, easy going, with smiling eyes and a certain shyness which people find endearing.

一九九七年十二月，在倫敦參加「辣妹世界」（Spiceworld）的首度演唱會。

一九九八年三月在加拿大溫哥華。

超級威廉旋風

　　一九九八年三月，威廉王子和弟弟哈利王子陪著他們的父親，到英屬哥倫比亞度過他們私人的家庭滑雪假期。在這趟假期之前，他們也隨著父親在加拿大參與一些皇室的義務列席會。但絕不會有人料到威廉的到來，竟然在當地掀起了一場「超級威廉旋風」。

　　面對加拿大那些為他瘋狂的少女們，起初威廉有點臉紅，覺得有些不習慣，但害羞的王子終於還是鼓起勇氣走出了飯店，去迎接那些欣喜若狂，為他深深著迷的少女們。他走過列隊歡迎他的群眾，並與她們一一握手，接受人群的尖叫歡呼與禮物，正如他廣受人民愛載的母親一般，表現得如此自然。

Blushing a little at first, and appearing somewhat diffident, the shy prince walked out of the hotel to a crescendo of screams and acclamation. Blushing openly he walked over to the lines of teenage girls who were waiting to see him and began shaking some by the hand, while, at the same accept gifts of be loved teddy bears which the girls gave him as heartfelt presents, openly declaring their loved and admiration. He responded as naturally as his mother responded to crowds of wellwishers and supporters; he smiled like a Hollywood actor, he answered their questions, shook their hands and took their gifts, thanking all of them. In tern, they responded by declaring undying love for him.

國家圖書館出版品預行編目資料

走出城堡的王子：William / 尼可拉斯.戴維斯(Nicholas Davies) 作；
柔之譯.
-- -- 初版. -- --
臺北市： 大都會文化,
2001〔民90〕
面； 公分

ISBN ：957-30552-3-6 (平裝)
1. 威廉(William, prince, grandson of Elizabeth II,
　 Queen of Great Britain, 1982-　) - 照片集

784.18　　　　　　　　　　　　　　　　　90008296

走出城堡的王子

作者	尼可拉斯.戴維斯
發行人	林敬彬
企劃主編	趙濰
執行編輯	方怡清
美術編輯	邱世珮
封面設計	邱世珮

出版發行	大都會文化事業有限公司
	110台北市基隆路一段432號4樓之9
讀者服務專線	（02）27235216
讀者服務傳真	（02）27235220
電子郵件信箱	metro@ms21.hinet.net
郵政劃撥帳號	14050529 大都會文化事業有限公司

港澳地區經銷	全力圖書有限公司
聯絡地址	香港新界葵涌打磚坪街58-76號　和豐工業中心1樓8室
聯絡電話	（852）24947282
聯絡傳真	（852）24947609

出版日期	2001年7月初版第1刷
定價	160元

ISBN	957-30552-3-6
書號	98007

Printed in Taiwan.

William Arthur Philip Louis

William Arthur Philip Louis

William Arthur Philip Louis

William Arthur Philip Louis

本圖摘自優雅與狂野一書　大旗出版，大都會文化發行

Not For Sale

本圖摘自優雅與狂野一書　大旗出版，大都會文化發行

Not For Sale

本圖摘自優雅與狂野一書　大旗出版，大都會文化發行

Not For Sale

本圖摘自優雅與狂野一書　大旗出版，大都會文化發行

Not For Sale